DIANE WAKOSKI
GREED
PARTS 5-7

BLACK SPARROW PRESS   LOS ANGELES 1971

PS
3573
A 42
G 7
pt. 5-7

5/1973
Sear

Black Sparrow Press
P.O. Box 25603
Los Angeles, California
90025

SBN 87685-094-8 (paper)
SBN 87685-095-6 (signed cloth)

GREED, PART 5

The Shark — Parents & Children

The Shark — Parents & Children

I can't swim.
I am afraid of water
    or
what lives in it.
I love the ocean.
I get seasick.
If I could choose one place in the world to live
it would be at the beach
even though
I can't swim.
I am afraid of water
      or
(fascinated by)
what lives in it.

I am trying to concentrate on my didactic feelings
about the shark.
From my encyclopedia I learn
about life
and as I read about the shark
my mind wanders/
                    stream of consciousness
      the water
        our tears
        amniotic fluid
my own children — a son
                a daughter
lost to me
me lost to them
forever
unless perhaps some day this tiger shark

floats down some river,
a message in a bottle gets to them
tells them
how much
I love the world,
the people in it,
how much I
don't want any of
                    them
to suffer
all the things I have had
to suffer.

Sacrifice.
That means giving up something.
No. That means giving up something which seems great
                in the eyes of the world
                in your eyes?
for something which seems
in a worldly sense
less
but in a spiritual sense
greater.
The idea is of spiritual returns.
Intangible ones.
I gave up my children when I was young
because I had no money,
no husband.
Children cannot understand or accept poverty
the way adults can.
They hate their parents,
but they need them.
Every child is damaged by his parents.

8

Every parent is damaged by his children.
Children are more damaged when they have only one parent
than two.
I gave up my children so that they could have
better parents
and not have to suffer poverty.
I gave up my children so that I could have all my time and
energy to be a person/a poet.
There should not be any sacrifice here.
That the children had to give up me
was no sacrifice because they got a complete set of parents,
better than I
and will never have to suffer poverty.
They gave up something small to get something big.
They gave up something emotional to get something material.
That's not sacrifice. That's reward.
I gave them up to achieve my soul, my life.
That's not small.
That's something big for something small.
None of you will understand this.
Unless you have divested yourself of sentimentality.
And most of you haven't done that.
Sacrifice is sentimental.

* *

Sharks are found in all seas
of the world & at
all depths.
        I dig down/ to all depths
the scuba diver,
the skin diver

(that lover
that black man
who comes up out of my heart
with a baby sand shark
       this funny face:
       it's no good to eat,
       won't hurt anyone
goes down/
      I come
  up
with memories like baby sand sharks
dangling in
my hands, wet, new born/ just caught
    all the ways that loving hurts people.
My parents
who could give me nothing
but piano lessons
who pulled me out
of their harmless genes

have I anything to
thank them for

but the gift of life?

This breath,
this water that runs silvery
thru my hair
glistening on my lips
that came out of my eyes
this ocean that holds my spongy brain.

I want to talk about
> the greed that makes a parent want a child.
> That makes a woman want to use her body
> as a stretched, swollen, lumpy pocket in an old
> worn coat,
> that makes a man want to see some squalling
> smelly inarticulate baby animal take his name
> and imitate his actions.

What is that greed?
That mirror.
That desire for repeating ourselves
stamping ourselves on the world? I see it
as an angel
or a devil
a salmon or a shark.
> > It could make
these same people
produce beautiful objects
benevolent institutions
or write books and religions.
> > But in most
it only produces
the common herd
> > children
> > > more likenesses
of ourselves.

I am not arguing
to depopulate the world
by the way.
> Am rather saying
that some greed for our own existence

11

our identities
produces both children
and civilization.
But a human child stays at home
with his creator
too long.
Imagine
      if every novelist rewrote his book for 18 years,
      every architect re-designed his building for 18 years,
      a president spent 18 years rewriting a bill before trying
      to get it passed,
      a cook worked 18 years on the same ingredients.
Absurd?
But there our analogies could start working.
      I want to go back to my book about sharks.
The shark lacks bone. Its skeleton is cartilaginous.
It also lacks an air bladder.
Its skin is covered with scales.
It has several sets of external and internal teeth.
It is carnivorous.
Has a well developed sense of smell.
It is stupid.
The fins are valued for soups and as aphrodisiacs.
Its liver is a valuable source of Vitamin A.
According to fossil evidence
sharks are primitive creatures

              Dogfish
              Hammerhead
              Macheral Shark
              Monkfish
              Porbeagle
              Thresher Shark
              Tiger Shark

Whale Shark

when I start listing beautiful names
it is because my own pain is so deep.

Do you know the story
of my life?
Everything is a distraction.
I am a fish swimming in mined waters.
I am a fish in water that has been torpedoed.
I am a fish in a volcanic ocean.

Oh, the detritus, the confusion, the noise, the floating anger.

I want to chronicle this story.
I have never told it before.
I wonder
if it is a story everyone knows?
One I tell,
inadvertently,
every day of my life.
I am arrested
by my fears, my stupidities, my failures,
and my attempt to turn these tormenting realities
into a structure of strength,
a moral argument,
a stern face.
Am I stupid, am I cruel, am I a shark too?
with a small brain, an instinct
for greed?
Am I the one thing man has to fear;
am I all a long bloated fallen
scarred ugly metaphor?

Hurt
hurt
hurt
I have been so
hurt.
How can I talk about my hurt.
I went swimming in shark infested waters
    sharks exploding like waterlilies to the surface,
    sharks like airplane pilots,
    on fire,
    sharks like acid eating my throat:
    my throat
          and I lost my legs
          I lost my arms,
          they are ladders of shale and lime, my voice
          is deserting me. I cannot talk
          under the water
          of my tears.
          There are old bones. They are older than any
          survivor of slavery.
Greed. I am talking about wanting more than
you have earned.
More than your life can support.
More than your body can digest, use, tolerate,
sustain.

This greed makes a man desire to extend his
definitions
in the world
by having children,
by making them extensions of himself.

This greed makes a man afraid of living his own life, all by himself, and gives him children to substitute for the areas of his life in which he fails. This greed makes a man, fearing failure, offer to the world these children as excuses, as hard work along the way, as digressions from his real work, as responsibilities that give him a valid excuse for not having the time or energy to succeed at the goals for himself.

(But what excuses do I practice?
What sharks live in my empty belly?)

Stop digressing,
I say to myself. Why aren't you saying
what you want to say? There's
no music here.
Only strong loud thuds that bang the piano keys,
crush the keyboard,
bloody.
Bloody fingers.
Smashed. No music. Sharks filling the water,
circling for my blood. The east river is in my house.
The ocean is in my ears.
The deaf man under my bloody face, my
hands, helpless, shame.
        The blood of shame.
        The blood of living without love.
        I am not noble.
        I am not strong.
        I did not give up my children for goodness; but
        because I was helpless,
        crushed, stupid,
        bloody, weak.
        And I would not criticize others now

15

who are not good parents,
who use their children as possessions,
who disguise their own failures with the accomplish-
ments of children,
who don't want children and so compete with them and
crush them,
who make weaklings to prove their own feeble strengths,
who try to validate their lives with carbon copies.
Forget all this. The bad bad parents.
Are there any good ones?
My grief is old and ugly.
The wounds on my belly

                 — like them
                 ugly wrinkled old lines.

Pain
pain
pain.
If
I say it again and again, will the pain
like sediment in the water
clear away
and leave me with a story I can understand?
A reality I can —

Stop talking.
You are blood
clouding the water.
You can only attract sharks.

Pain.
No man has wanted to spend his life with me.
The pain of sharks eating at my throat.
No man has asked me to share my life with him.

The pain of sharks eating at my lips.
No man has wanted to marry me.
The pain of sharks biting at my cheek.
No man has been willing to take care of me or give me a home.
The pain of sharks eating at my ridged, aching back.
Each vertebra a bullet. A lump of scar tissue.
A strength earned by sharks biting and making me
bleed.
   I could not stand up
         I grew new bones
I am a tower of ugly strength, this body
only the sharks have enjoyed.
No man has wanted my children.
Pain
pain.
The shame of being a woman
with a big belly
     and no man
     to claim the child.
Only the sharks.
Throw them my heart
as diversion.
The pain of my shark-eaten heart.
The pain of bleeding and being unnamed.

This could not be a statement about greed.
It is about pain.
My pain.
Pain
pain.
My weeping from
pain.
The greed I have tried to understand in others/

not those who feel pain
but those who create it.

And the pain
I know
my own children
my son
my daughter
must feel not knowing why they have different parents
than the ones they were born to.
They will trouble themselves with grief
asking why
over and over
their mother,
their father
did not want them. Searching for some secret flaw,
some insignificance which will torture them
at night.
Just as I torture myself again and again
with the question: what was wrong with me? Why
has no man ever wanted me
and my children,
even now
that I am old and past such desires,
when words are more to me
than flesh could ever be,
yet I
like every woman
must ask myself
those questions, and when I do
my shoulders lift out of the water
dazzled
surrounded

by the mouths waiting to tear apart
my flesh.
It is a cold and hungry world.
There is only one thing you can honor a man for:
transforming his suffering into something beautiful —
Beethoven
my inspiration
the only thing which forgives my fevers,
would not
however,
prevent a shark
from tearing any of us apart.
Yet I would prefer Beethoven
to a competing pair/   of teeth.
We are all sharks.
The only question will be
                   whose flesh
will we strip
bloody and raw
from the bones?
Will it be our children's
or our own
or some poor stranger who comes by
when we are hungry
and it is time
for another cold meal?

GREED, PART 6

Jealousy — A Confessional

Jealousy — A Confessional

This poem is dedicated to Humphrey Bogart in *The African Queen* who knew how to pick the leeches off. "Nasty things," he called them.

They are black,
and they gleam like Steinways.

28 May 1970

Dear Diary:

For the past few months these feelings have been exploding inside me, giving me a sore throat with all the angry words I have held back and not said, giving me a sense of heaviness, as if my veins were gorged with blood or some poisonous liquid, and making people keep away from me for the angry things that have overflowed and poured out of me, despite my attempts to remain controlled.

These feelings are too immediate, intense, and especially too petty and mean to make poetry or art from. And I do not believe psychiatrists or religion help one much — at least not one like me who fights off all authority figures as if they were alligators trying to snip off an arm or leg.

The terrible thing about these feelings is that they have invaded both my personal and my professional life, and they are attacking me, like a school of sharks, all at once, in every vital area trying to destroy everything that is decent and generous and high-minded about me.

Those are qualities, by the way, that I've always prided myself on. Decency — behaving well and honestly, with fairness towards other people. And generosity — since I myself have been so

23

afflicted by the stinginess of the world. And, of course, high mindedness — why else have I lived a life with so few material or tangible rewards, other than that I believe in honesty and courage and virtue; will not be hypocritical for the small amounts of harmony it temporarily distills.

But now, this jealousy is sucking away at me, like leeches, and threatening to leave a poisoned, feeble animal behind. There is no woman I meet who I feel isn't trying to steal the man I love away from me. By being more beautiful. By acting more intelligent. By having more money or talent. There is no poet I meet who I feel hasn't stolen bread out of my mouth by winning a grant, a prize, a reading or recording that I didn't get. I never read a review any more without feeling that my work is more worth talking about than whoever is being reviewed. I never hear praise of anyone else without wanting to kill or destroy them. I see every wealthy person as having wealth I should have had. I see every married woman as a living symbol to remind me that I am unmarried and unmarriageable. I see every beautiful face as a reminder of my plain one. I see in fact anything which I have tried to associate myself with — even ideas — as my 33 year old possessions and begin to feel drained, sucked dry, leeched out, the minute anyone else participates even for a minute in them.

I guess jealousy must come out first, greedily narcissistically making a person or an intangible idea of something into a possession, and then having done so, constantly feeling that it will be stolen away from you. Sometimes, and this is when the jealousy is worst, it is something you have never had at all; but thought you deserved it more than whoever had it (an award, an honor, money, someone you love who doesn't love you?) and then the jealousy is rampant and unrelenting and it is like having leeches on every part of you, from the soft spots between your toes, to the inner fatty thighs, through the soft belly and armpits, to the neck, trying for the eyes, eager for the brain.

This is sheer confession, by the way. I am talking about it for one simple reason: so that you will know about it. And it is trying to kill me, and these may be my last words on the subject. There is no poetry for it. Those blood suckers have done their work inside this blood factory, and killed any of the energy that make a beautiful song, lament, argument, narrative or portrait. I don't even ask you to forgive me or be indulgent. There is ugliness and madness here, and while these leeches are present, no decency can exist. Perhaps I believe in exorcism. Oh, obviously I do believe in exorcism or at least catharsis, and that is my purpose too in writing all this out. To clean myself out. To get rid of it. But I wonder? You've heard of people being operated on for cancer — the surgeon opening them up and seeing those deadly extra cells cropping out everywhere like friends at a surprise party — behind the chairs and sofas and pianos in a seemingly empty room.

Or have you ever opened a piece of fruit or an ear of corn and found it full of worms. And they wake me up in the middle of the night, as they did last night, screaming for blood. Leaving me bursting with some indefinable feeling and a need to scream very very loud.

This is not a sudden disease. One leech doesn't do you in. But something that builds. Something that is applied over and over. The "medicinal" leech that is applied each day — until too much blood is gone. So I know it didn't happen overnight. It's not like food poisoning that you can trace to one guilty piece of meat; a bubonic plague to some innocent rat harboring the lethal fleas. No. If it's hit me in epidemic proportion this year — this case of greedy hungry jealousy — then it's been there growing for a long time.

But I *can* pinpoint its power. I can tell you when those fires that burn as fever in me got inflamed and started that hard fast burning that leaves me pale and weak and petty — oh, so petty and mean and unworthy for the next few days.

I don't know why I'm putting all this down actually. I don't know why I'm confessing all these things to you. Oh yes, I said before that I believed in exorcism. And I'm trying to get rid of my demons. But why am I telling you? Why do I think you should be interested? Well, I guess I'm telling you because there can be no confession without an audience to confess to. Someone to hear you, to sigh for the human condition, be angry at evil, and then wave his hand in the air and feel that he knows more about life. I suppose I think you'll be interested because madness always interests others a bit and some of you probably will feel that I'm talking, even, about your own madness and wonder if perhaps I'll give you any insights into your own ways. Any answers. But I am angry at myself that I can't get this into lines, instead of sentences, that my metaphor of the leeches isn't more profound or inventive, that I don't have more images to dazzle you with, or more universal experiences to talk about. And I love ironies. So my favorite thing to do would be to write a long poem despising and putting down Pulitzer Prizes and then win one for it. But, critics, when you read this, I don't for once want you to review it; I want you to review yourselves and learn not about literature, but about life — how goodness, or the desire for it drives us mad. And, of course, I want you to reflect on those who are still sane — from innocence or evil. And think a while about them both — the innocent and the evil.

26

Last night: why did I wake up last night with a strange feeling — alone, wondering if you were with some other woman, having dreamed this:

> My mother was my husband's (in the dream) first wife. In real life I don't have a husband. In real life my mother has white hair. Had white hair at the age of 32 when I, her first child, was born. Her father, my maternal grandfather, had white hair at the age of 30. I am now 32, the age my mother was when I was born, and I have blond hair with a lot of silvery-grey strands in it. Anyway, in the dream, my mother had long silver-white hair, and when she died my husband scalped her and kept the long silver-blond hair in a wooden box. He took it out often during the dream, combed and admired it, and at one point, even, cut it. During the dream, there was a car ride in which someone was chasing us to prove that we had stolen a case of peas from the A & P. I was angry at my husband because he kept stopping the car to comb and admire my mother's scalp.

Anyway, I woke up suddenly thinking I must either call or write you, Tony, and demand 3 things. Fortunately I curbed myself, got a drink of water, read a John Cheever story, turned over on my belly, turned out the light, and made myself go back to sleep by thinking of all the different ways an ocean can look from a cliff-ish beach. I felt, when I woke up, however, that I had to demand three things from you. And, in spite of the favorable fact that I have not demanded them, they still haunt me. I felt I had to demand that you tell me what girl you had with you last February when I came to your apartment where we had lived together for a year and a half, after you had thrown me out a week before, saying you wanted to be alone. Remember when I came and found the upper dead bolt locked? Is that really the name of the lock I wonder — "dead bolt" — or did I make that up to fit my feelings? Writing a poem about that day — a good poem — has never exorcised the image of that girl's leather purse left on your couch, the closed bedroom door and the look on your face when I asked you if there was a girl in there. And it sometimes worries me so much, wondering who she was and why you wanted her and not me, that I can't move or think. Why didn't you want me? Why did you want her? I guess I had been dreaming, actually, that I came home and that dead bolt was on. I woke up being more jealous of that girl than of the fact that you had once married someone else.

The second thing I woke up feeling I had to demand from you, Tony, was the name of that blond girl whose photograph you had in your bedroom when we got back together this winter. The one you took with you to Vermont last summer and whom you must have treated as your girlfriend — am I anything more? — for a while. Why I want to know her name is a mystery even to me. Surely I don't want to go out and murder her, though at times I easily could. Why should I want to make her life miserable? That is past. You spend your time with me. But she is still, the idea of her is still, an affront to me. Someone you *preferred* to me. I could never feel this way about women you were involved with before I knew you. But this is different. You had thrown me out of your house. Out of your life. You had rejected me. And she is someone you took in preference to me. That will always be a memory that hurts.

There's the jealousy. You are, of course, not my possession, though I always think of myself as yours. Perhaps because I am a "possessed" woman and prefer to think of you possessing me

28

than some devil. Even though you are not/cannot/I would not want you to be my possession, I suppose I think of love as possessing. And the idea that you let someone else possess you in preference to me drives me into a fury, as if someone had stolen one of my poems and said he had written it. There, you see. Petty. Small. Ungenerous. Besides the basic flaw of thinking of persons as possessions, the real human failing is being ungenerous with those possessions. How I hate myself for that. Pettiness is a trait I cannot tolerate. It is the source of evil. Not power, as some people say. Power only augments evil. Pettiness creates it.

And the third thing that I was going to demand of you was that you marry me. But I have no rights there. That you care for me, I know. What difference should it really make if the world knows it or not? For me, crazy and mixed up on the subject of possessions marriage is the symbol that a man cares enough for a woman to let the world know about it. Anything other than marriage is their private arrangement, their temporary, though often passionate or fine, feeling for each other. When you marry, you say to everybody, this woman is the one I prefer. Again, here is a pettiness on my part. Why should I care if the world thinks no one cares for me? Is it that I feel so small and insignificant that I cannot imagine anyone thinking that anyone else could care for me?

Well, anyway, I didn't call you or write a letter demanding any of those things. And that is why I must write them as part of a confessional this morning, and while I know it is still petty and weak of me to need to do this, at least it is not so very ungenerous and indecent of me as burdening you with the responsibility for my torment would have been.

There is a man I've met a few times, actually whom I like. The idea of his money has sucked at me in every spot until I am weak and foolish on the subject of money; or money and people with it; or money and artists; or maybe it's money and me. Anyway, I am terribly jealous of this man's income and spend hours wondering about how to make money myself. And yet, it seems obvious that money is not my main concern or I would not be so careless with it, nor would I have chosen to become a poet — surely a profession which never creates millionaires. The idea of a man, heir to millions, who has a $300,000 a year income and who writes poetry which doesn't deal with what surely must be the paramount experience of his young life — what it means to be wealthy — angers me. In my jealousy I see him with his young, unformed poetry taking away my jobs, my reputation, my publishers, winning prizes I never win, and being paid more for poetry readings than I am. In the abstract, or when I see him, I like him; perhaps am even a little in love with him. But the vision of his $300,000 lowers down over my head like a safe coming out of a 10th story window, crashes on me, and I feel the little mouths of those leeches biting down, beginning to drain my color, taking all my courage and energy from me. Making me into a bitter, aging, nasty woman.

I am very melodramatic. I see myself hanging on a cross, with nails gouging out the thick flesh of the feet and pulling through the bloody tendons and delicate bones of the hands. "Poetry where are you," I say, feeling that most of the men and women who call themselves poets are idle dumb fools with tin ears and petty lives. I hate myself for being so small, so unfeeling, and for smiling at these people weakly instead of snarling, if indeed that is really the way I feel. My sins get larger every day. I take a breath and realize I am not only mean and ungenerous but also a hypocrite about it. I start with lack of generosity, an unwillingness to appreciate others, descend to pettiness in making nasty comments about them or their lives and works, and end, compounding my ugly greed, by being hypocritical and smiling at them when they pass by. These are sins nothing can absolve me from. Ones that can only be mended by becoming first an honest person, and then trying to regain some of my original generosity and decency towards others. But is there any left in me? Or have I been sucked dry? Each year of poverty has taken its toll.

Each year when I was ignored and others far less capable or interesting were praised. Each year I applied for something and my forms were returned with a printed rejection. Each time the man I loved betrayed me with another woman or refused to marry me or threw me out, saying he wanted to be alone. Each time I was scorned in some way, when something, as I saw it, which belonged to me was taken away and given to someone else.

A good man is one who sees no cause for bitterness in this. Who does not find himself demeaned or hurt by such things. But what is it that protects him, keeps him whole, gives him transfusions of plasma to replace his evaporating blood?

Perhaps faith in himself? A belief that art or love or anything valuable and beautiful is beyond the temporal?

Whatever it is, it is feeble and ill in me. I am a transplanted tree, elm, oak, some hard wood, at the droopy stage. Will my melodramatic roots, that in my former location nourished me, take hold in this new space and grow?

I cannot continue this confessional. Here is a poem:

That Delicate Reptile

There is a small pink coral snake
like the ring of a Countess
curled up
in my brain, eating it away.
I keep finding real reasons
like birds that fly out of a tree, a cloud of them, when you walk
under it,
for why I am angry,
hurt,
unsatisfied,
but all the time it is that snake eating morsels
of the brain, expanding
a little to take
a bigger place there,
sliding his body, with each scale rippling
                    like a blood transfusion
to move
into a newer
thicker
coil.
        My neck aches
unbearably; to carry anything
is torture, though I do it out of a sense of
human responsibility; when I tilt my head,
I lose my balance
and feel as if I had been eating snakes.
Oh, that small dainty reptile
that bracelet
coral as a rabbit's eye

the size of a thermometer,
is slowly replacing my brain. The angers I feel
are poisonous and bitter;
the love I feel unsteady and frightened as though
treachery were a norm;
and these pains through the trunk of my neck
penetrating the backs of my ears,
remind me
of that delicate snake
which has lodged itself there.
I have always been
a good neighbor;
but his eyes tell me,
gleaming like two pinholes in a dark curtain
that he does not much care for
old rules.
I sit down to smoke, but a nudging
behind my ears
signals
that if I were prudent
I'd stop.
I try to quote a line of poetry. Something about
good fences
and realize it doesn't apply.
His being in my brain
it being his living room, so to speak —
I wonder now
about his name.
But
this is a little late
for such preliminaries. I sit still
and wonder
when will he decide

to make himself known
to the world?

Will I,
do you suppose,
have my choice
of being deadly
or
dead?

GREED, PART 7

Self-Righteousness

Self-Righteousness

"Pride goeth before a fall,"
repeated my mother
self-righteously to her children. "Pride
goeth before a fall,"
I repeated to myself,
though it was much more likely
I would stumble and fall
because I was near-sighted and couldn't see,
much more likely I would fall
because the porch steps were broken
or because I was clumsy and ashamed of my body
and afraid of my life.
But I was different,
quiet,
my face turned red
when spoken to,
                    and I was proud,
proud, proud,
like some beautiful creature deep in the ocean,
dug into the underwater caverns
moving slowly
through gorgonians, sea fans,
spreading over the breathing walls,
aloof,
unexploited.
I was a little ocean named Diane,
a coral reef,
a sea anemone,
a chambered nautilus,
glowing with possibilities no one knew.
"Pride," my mother

would whisper,
as I played the piano,
as I sped through school books with lightning speed,
oh the light of the underwater
world,
glinting,
reflected, inside my own head I was
the Lion Fish of Saudi Arabia,
swimming slowly through the Red Sea,
long spines,
like files,
or the rails from spiral iron stairs,
stick up in a fan,
a mane,
over my body.
Their poison is more deadly
than the bite of a cobra,
my fins are angry too,
slowly they open and shut,
seeming to breathe,
and I move wherever I want to go,
unharmed and beautiful
because
deadly.
          The Lion Fish
born in the constellation of that roaring beast,
blundering through the summer sky,
pausing on my own porch steps to hear my mother say,
"pride
goeth before a fall,"
and looking grimly at me,
saying she hoped my life was better than
hers,

         pride
she seemed to whisper,
making me hunch my already-round shoulders,
lowering my eyes,
my face turning as red as the Lion Fish
a kind of lobster king,
arms stiff with anger
when anyone looked at me.
What destiny is there
in the ocean;
it follows me,
the fire,
moving through water.
Pride holds my tongue,
makes me stammer,
gives me insufficient wit;
pride makes me grovel in shame when I see the
pride in others that is
ugly,
the self-righteous smugness
of safety, assurance,
the feeling that there are no mistakes;
pride makes me immodest when I compare myself
to less beautiful,
less deadly
creatures of the sea
                    even the sharks steer clear of me . . .
But pride is not
a source of shame,
of ugliness
or hurt
in human lives. Pride is
what gives us dignity,

even when we fall.
Oh, my mother, whispering to me,
who knows why,
making me ashamed of anything I could do,
making me afraid to assert myself
or to claim my rights.
Pride
is not
to be ashamed of.
>   But it is related to that deadly Lion Fish
we should all fear;
self-satisfaction,
self-righteousness,
smugness
and the anger that goes with it,
the willingness to say you are right
everyone else wrong.
>   There burn the fires of the Inquisition.
Self-righteousness makes truth,
honesty, goodness,
honorable actions — all of them
the victims of themselves. The fires that burn in me
when I am right
and the whole world is wrong,
when, in spite of temptation and torture
I have done the decent good thing
and everything else around me is corrupt
and corruptly perpetuating itself,
and I see this
and I start burning inside
with my rightness,
at that point I am ready to
forego

everything truth, honesty, goodness, and honorable actions
stand for,
and be carried away into the anger of the
righteous,
and from there,
comes vanity,
selfishness,
uncharitableness,
the angers that feed vengeance.
From purity, the transposition to corruption,
and all because the world does not often
honor
goodness
and unless we do, so much,
in our own minds,
then leading a good life
will make us angry
vengeful men.

Mother,
you whisperer of mottos
and guidelines,
you painful lesson in innocent evil,
it is not "pride that goeth before"
all my falls
but pride in what is right and good that picks me up
when I do fall;
pride, dignity,
faith in myself that allows me to realize how badly I
have acted some times
and not to be callous about changing
for the better.
You,

41

you reminder in the dark
of your own failings and hoping I would fail
too, you weak plunderer of children
in the name of goodness
and righteousness, with your "pride goeth before a fall"s,
and your "cleanliness is next to godliness"es and
other more secret doctrines,
                like "lay low for meddlers"
                the poetry of childhood,
smugly sitting there feeling
the world was doing you in,
self-righteously sitting there
hoping they would martyr you and you would be innocent,
oh the perils of perverse Christianity,
welcoming grief and oppression
rather than learning to fight them and only to submit
when there were no other alternatives.
Oh you false teacher,
letting me think if I were honest
and clean and straight,
the world would just be all right,
and that if it weren't I could sit righteously
in my chair of innocence and look back
at it
and somehow triumph.
But the world only admits it is wrong,
when you make it admit it is wrong;
and where is the poetry in that?

I have never been under the sea,
though photographs serve nicely to prick and pull
at my imagination.
This Lion Fish, which I have only seen on film,

is a magnificent creature,
living in very deep waters,
and it is a testimony to my history
that poisonous living things fascinate me,
the beautiful fin-spikes this fish wears like a mane,
the knives of 90 feet below,
with their Borgia touch,
what I would give to float so serenely through the world,
radiating the power that poison gives.
For the poison I know in my life
is poison that poisons me; the fire I know burns me
up; water drowns me and my fingers are not ice to others,
but their very touch freezes me.
I have walked so innocent,
for so many years,
and it is my own innocence that turns on me.
I have walked straight and honestly for so many years,
and it is my own honesty that
turns on me.
The men I loved so single-mindedly, so passionately,
so without guile —
they were frightened and angered and burdened by that very
single-mindedness, that passion,
that honesty.
The world I love,
full of artists, listening to their own sirens,
wailing in caverns under the water or
in a drum that beats behind some impenetrable wall,
they who roar like lions and live in the back of printing presses,
or those whose paint brushes are soaked
with sunlight, painting canvases with invisible elements
of piracy, the rare spices and gold brought from great distances,
that world I have asked so much of:

purity,
honesty,
recognition of true beauty,
art rather than deception,
imagination rather than guile,
that world where I've walked
worked
never trying to deceive,
always trying to give fair measure for what I take/

but to then expect that world to be as straight
and simple, as I see myself,
when it's older and more complex and
considerably different
from me —
a simple notion,
one that innocence can support.
But when innocence goes,
      — to school or to work —
simplicity is no substitute for intelligence.

My mother made me a breeding ground for
self-righteous anger.
It fermented in me like beer in an oak keg.
It ripened like Camembert,
it rose like yeast in good bread.
But I did not become a good meal of bread and beer and cheese.
I became an angry woman,
innocent only in my foolishness,
and the anger and vengeance nearly burned me up.
Not one corrupt hair of anyone I hated, or any air-conditioned
room of any falsely administered institution
caught on fire, got singed,

or even felt my own heat.
I was a bird caught in an oil slick from industrial nations.
I was a fish contaminated with 10 parts of mercury per 1000
in my guts.
I was a child playing in a field sprayed with parathion.
I was the side of a hill wrecked with open-pit mining.
I was Joan of Arc, a stubborn girl burned wastefully at the stake.
I was not a reformer.
I was not the reliever of corruption.
I was not even the means of success,
nor will I ever be.
My angers come from having lived as I was taught
and not feeling the world honors or
rewards me for any of my decency.
This anger has made me hard
and harsh
vain
unable to accept other people's success,
unable to believe any one else is honest,
though in my angers I have learned to be
dishonest,
unable to think of intrinsic rewards and merits,
taught me to be greedy and foolish and most of all,
bloodthirsty for vengeance on all
who have won false rewards.
The self-righteous executioner, I stand ready
to chop heads, hang weak men
and electrocute my detractors. There is no virtue here,
where my mother's anger burns,
whispering "pride goeth before a fall," and holding out
an ancient foot to trip all who pass before me.
Not pride,
not pride

45

which may heal us
and take us away from false issues
and impossible goals.
That Lion Fish,
that natural arsenal,
equipped for destruction —
self-righteousness,
the greedy thought that when you are right
you can burn others for their wrongness;
it is a fire that could destroy
the world.
It takes poets and holy men with it,
along with philosophers, scientists, parents,
and statesmen.
The mad bombers.
The Wars to End all Wars.
Remember the Lion Fish from the Red Sea —
its beauty,
its poison,

why should we touch it?

Diane Wakoski was born in California in 1937. Her published books, which give all the important information about her life, are *Coins & Coffins, Discrepancies and Apparitions, Greed, Parts 1 & 2, The George Washington Poems, Inside The Blood Factory, The Diamond Merchant, Thanking My Mother For Piano Lessons, Greed, Parts 3 & 4, The Moon Has A Complicated Geography, The Magellanic Clouds,* and *The Lament Of The Lady Bank Dick.*